Nonno Feels Young Again

By Clem King

It’s Nonno’s birthday today.
He’s eighty!

Nonno thinks we will just have a quiet dinner.
He does not know that everyone in his family is coming for a big party!

Having everyone in our home will be a tight fit.
I hope we have enough room!

Some people are coming from other countries for Nonno's party.

Cousin Enzo is flying all the way from southern Italy!
His plane will touch down soon.

Aunty Angela and Uncle Doug are driving from the countryside.

Uncle Doug calls to say they are stuck in traffic on the freeway, so they might be late.

Dad wants the house to look nice.

I encourage him to tie a huge red ribbon around the door for a fancy flourish.
It looks great!

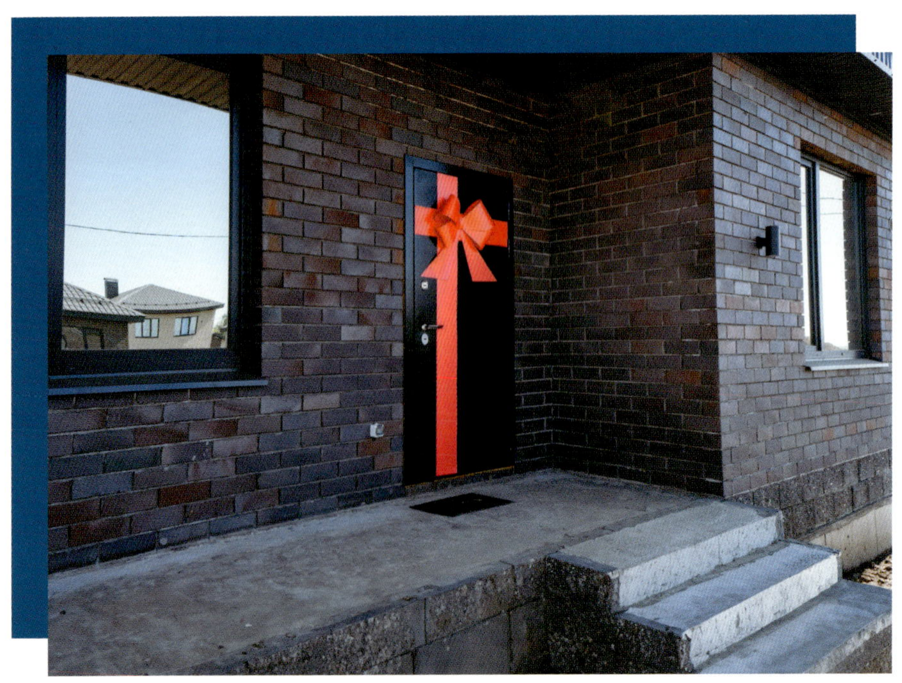

Then the family starts to arrive.

Uncle Doug and Aunty Angela are right on time!

Everyone brings birthday gifts for Nonno.

I make a big pile in the living room.

My little brother helps, but he's not tall enough to reach the top!

Nonno is **so** surprised to see everyone!

Nonno gives Nonna a big kiss!

“I’m so touched that you threw this party!” he tells her.

As the daylight fades, Mum lights some candles.

It's a cosy touch!

We all sit down to eat some nourishing food.

Dad serves up some chicken. He made lots of pasta and veggies, too.

Yum!

Then Mum gets the pie.

She was afraid there would not be enough food for everyone, but there is plenty!

It’s Nonno’s birthday, so we all encourage him to have the last slice of pie!

Nonno is so touched that everyone came to help him celebrate.

"I feel young again!" he says.

CHECKING FOR MEANING

1. Where is Cousin Enzo coming from? *(Literal)*
2. Who arrived right on time? *(Literal)*
3. How do you think Nonno felt on his big night? *(Inferential)*
4. Nonno's big birthday celebration was a surprise party. Do you think that made it more special for Nonno? Why? *(Evaluative)*

EXTENDING VOCABULARY

flourish	A flourish is an extra detail or decoration used to make something a bit more special, like putting a ribbon on the door. What other kinds of flourishes can you think of?
touched	When Nonno says *"I'm so touched"*, what does he mean? How does he feel?
nourishing	What does it mean if food is nourishing? Is it good for you? In what ways?

MOVING BEYOND THE TEXT

1. Enzo flew to the party from Italy, and Aunty Angela and Uncle Doug drove from the countryside. What are some other ways you could travel to a celebration?
2. The family celebrated Nonno's 80th birthday. What other big events or accomplishments do people like to celebrate? Why?
3. Who would you invite if you were planning an important celebration?
4. Nonno had chicken, pasta and pie at his party. What kinds of foods would you like to have at a party or special event?

TIME TO WRITE

Write about your perfect birthday party. Who would you invite? What food would you have? What games would you play?